Riding Hood
©2016 by Silvana Soriano
"As once the winged energy of delight"
poem by Rainer Maria Rilke
Illustration Silvana Soriano

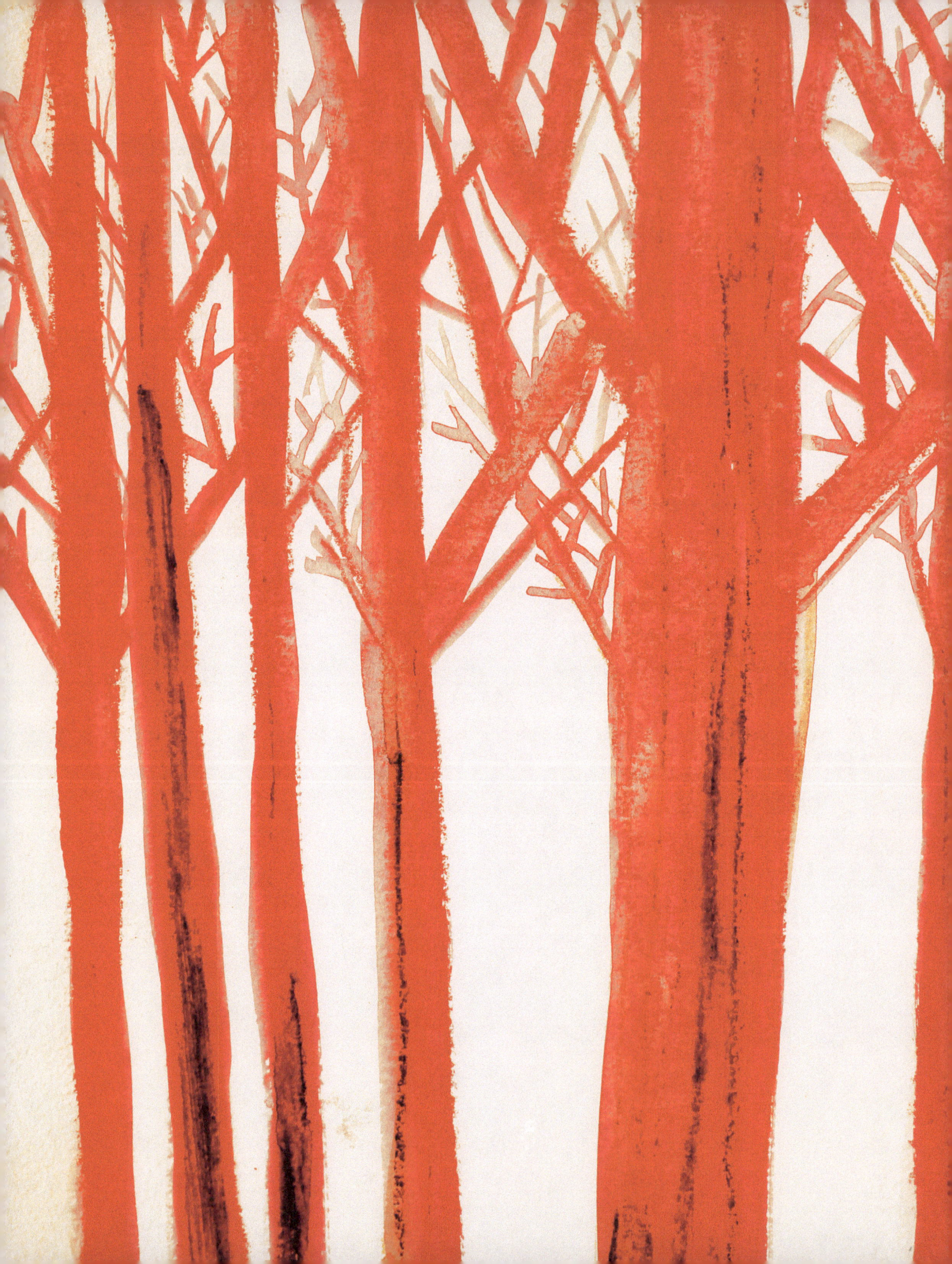

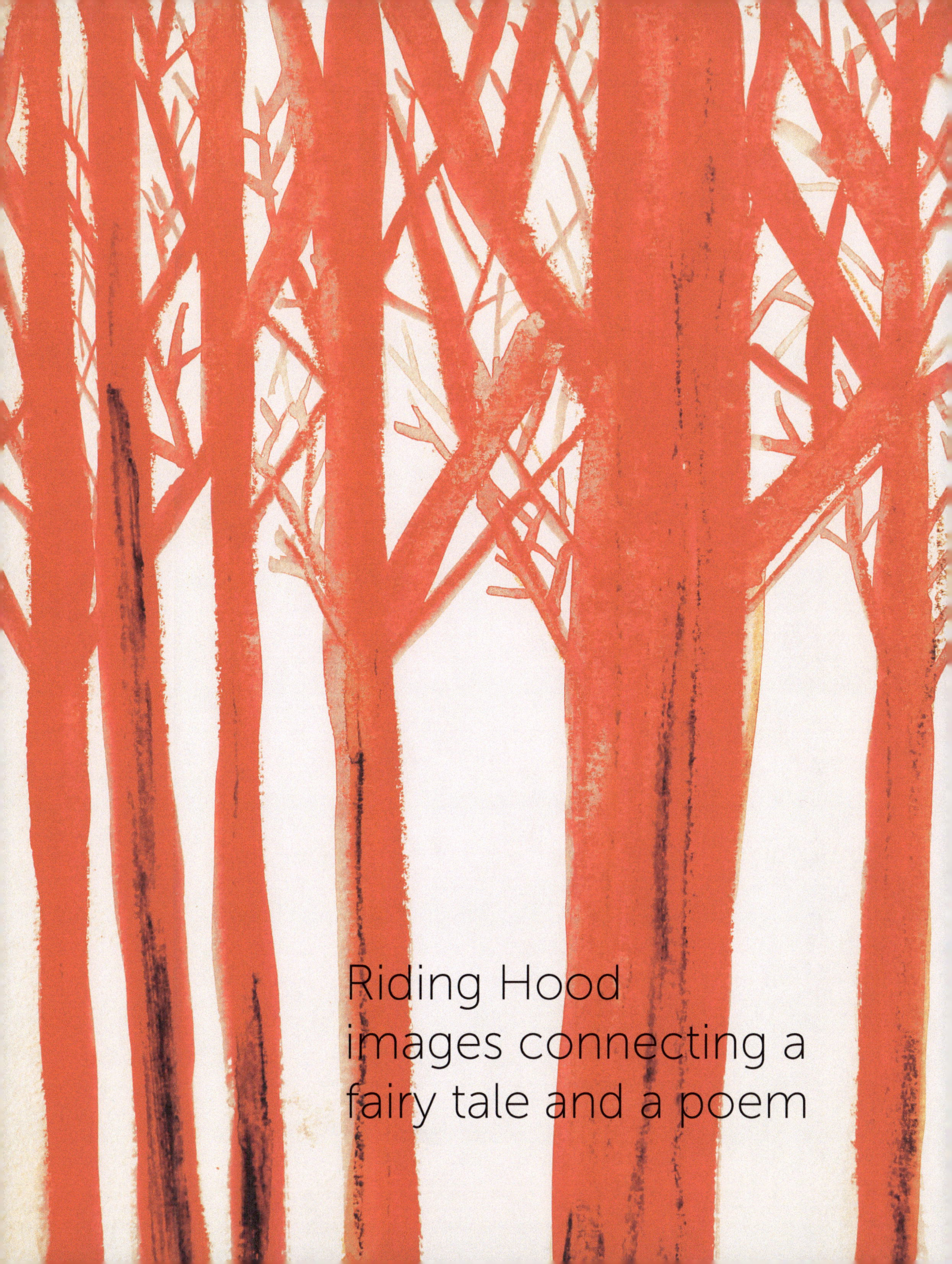

Riding Hood
images connecting a
fairy tale and a poem

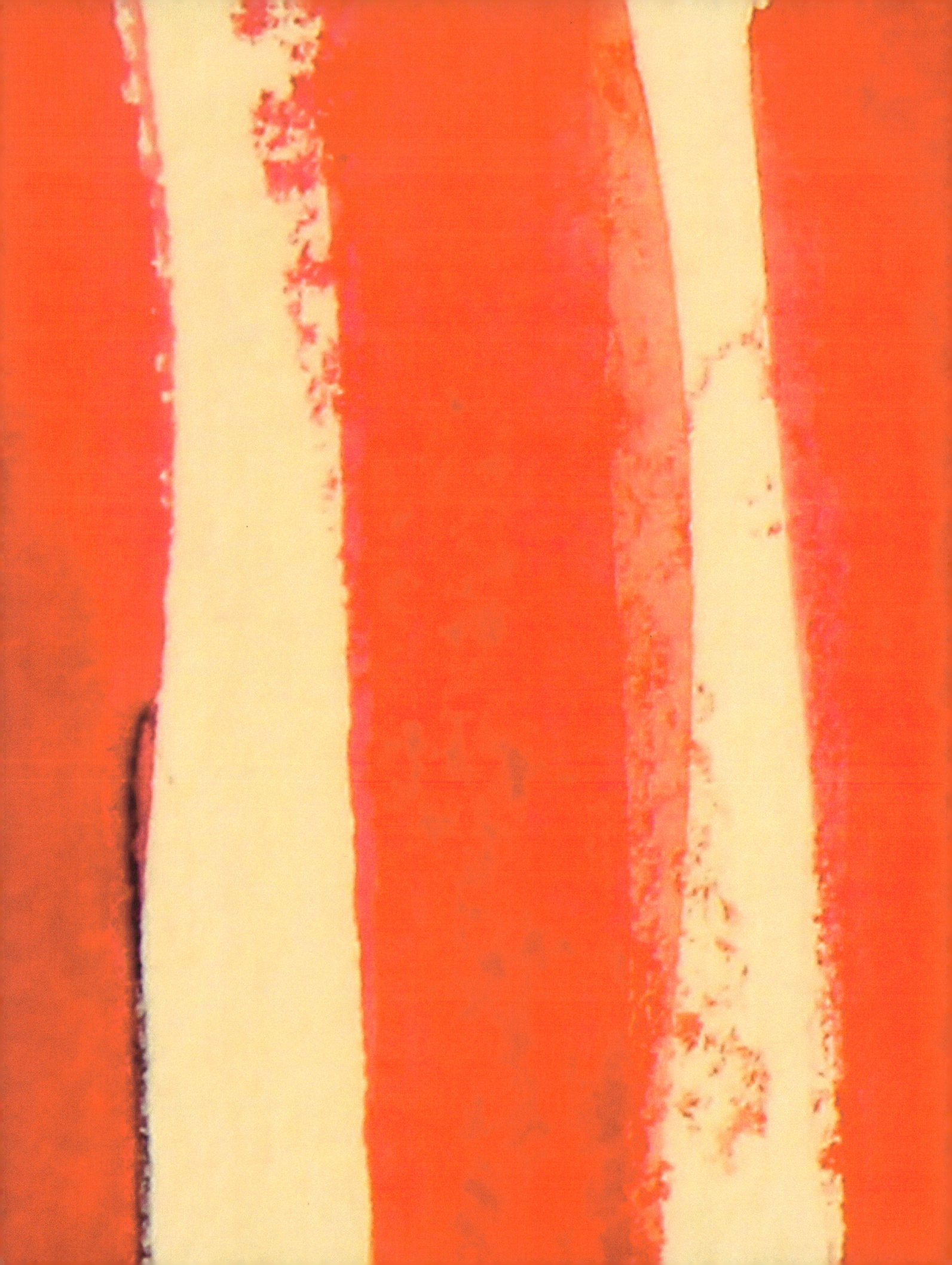

Rainer Maria Rilke & Little Red Riding Hood
My favorite poet and fairy tale

a Homage to
Sofia Giodarnni and Sofia Soriano

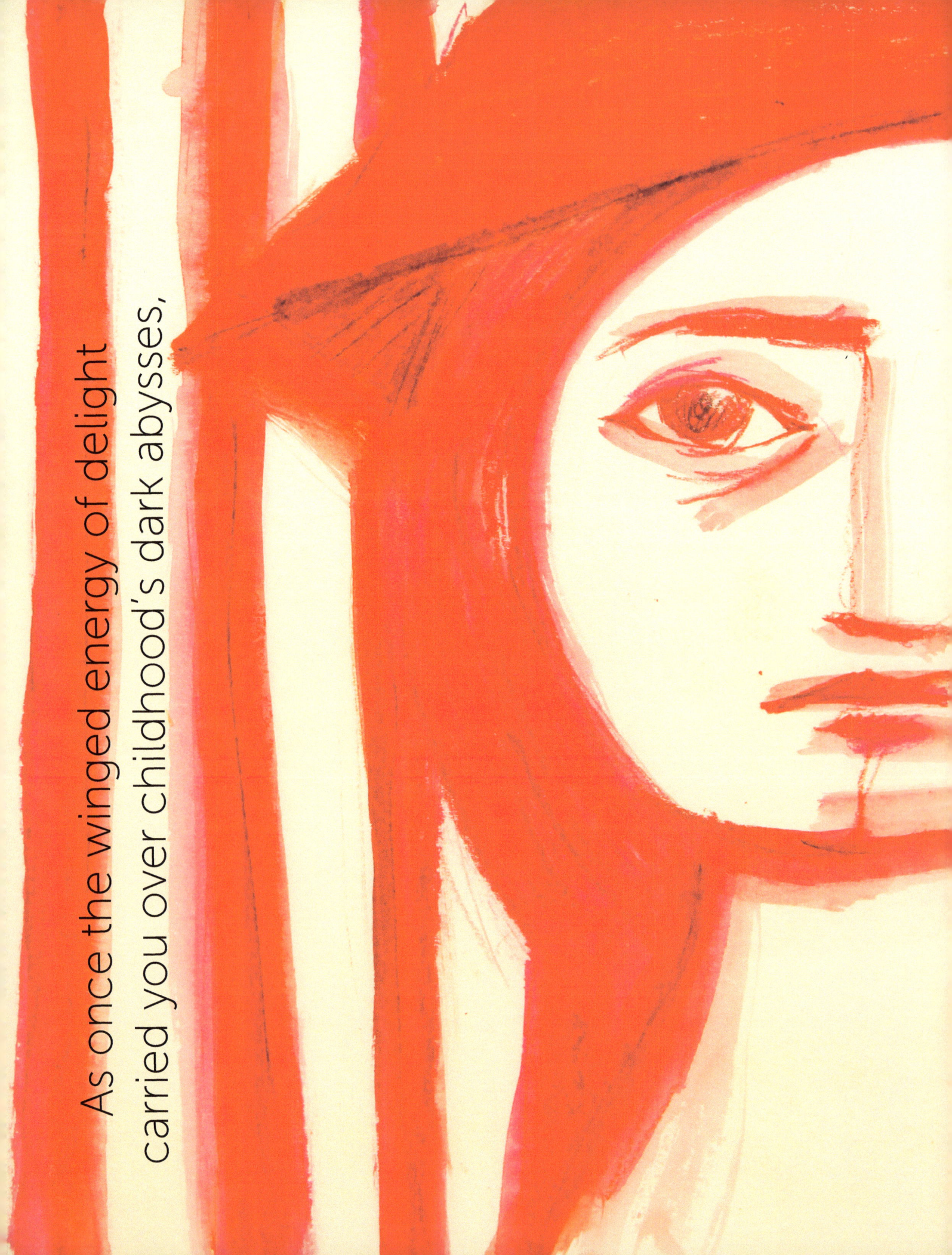

As once the winged energy of delight
carried you over childhood's dark abysses,

now beyond your own life build the great arch of unimagined bridges.

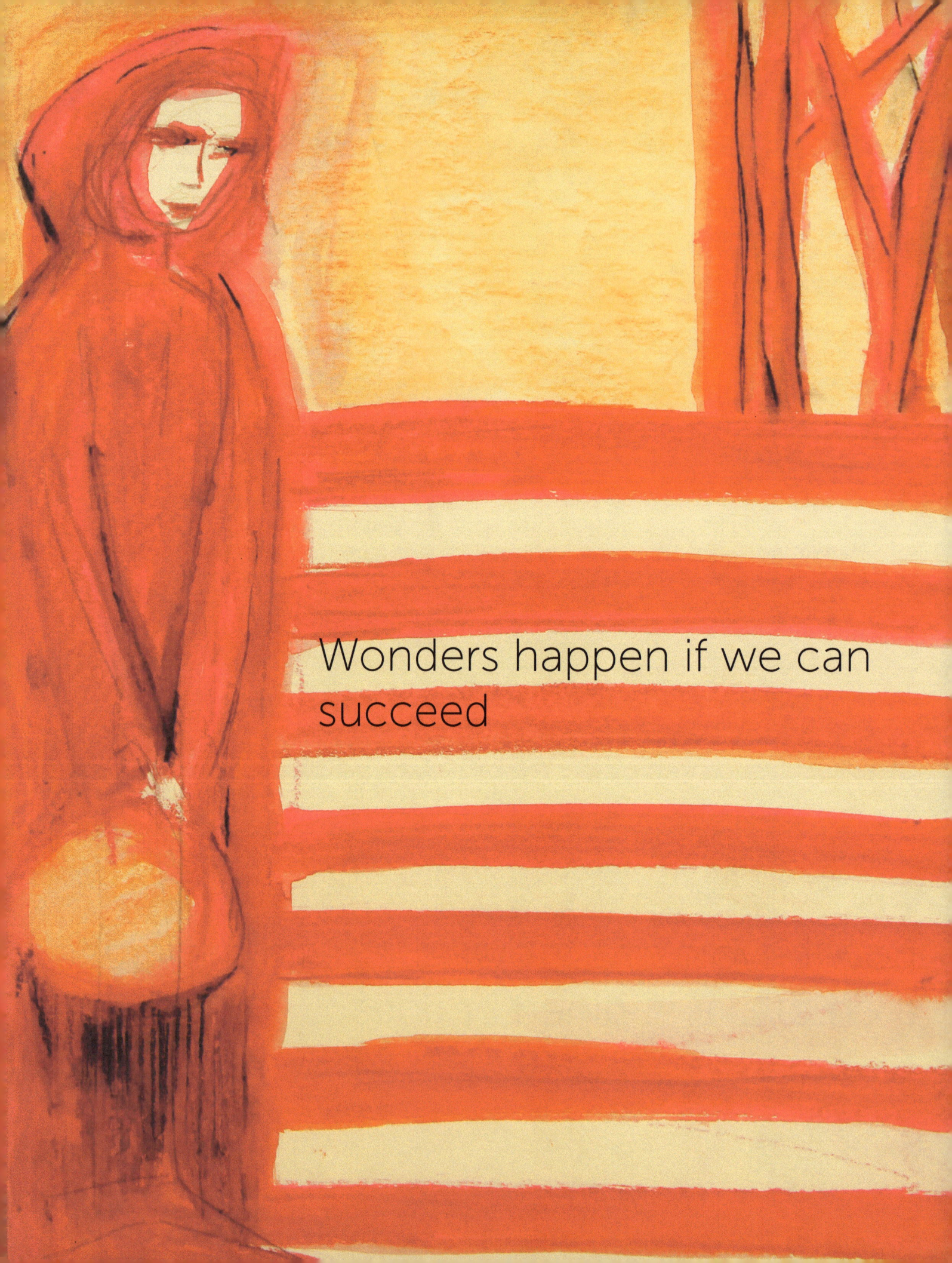

Wonders happen if we can succeed

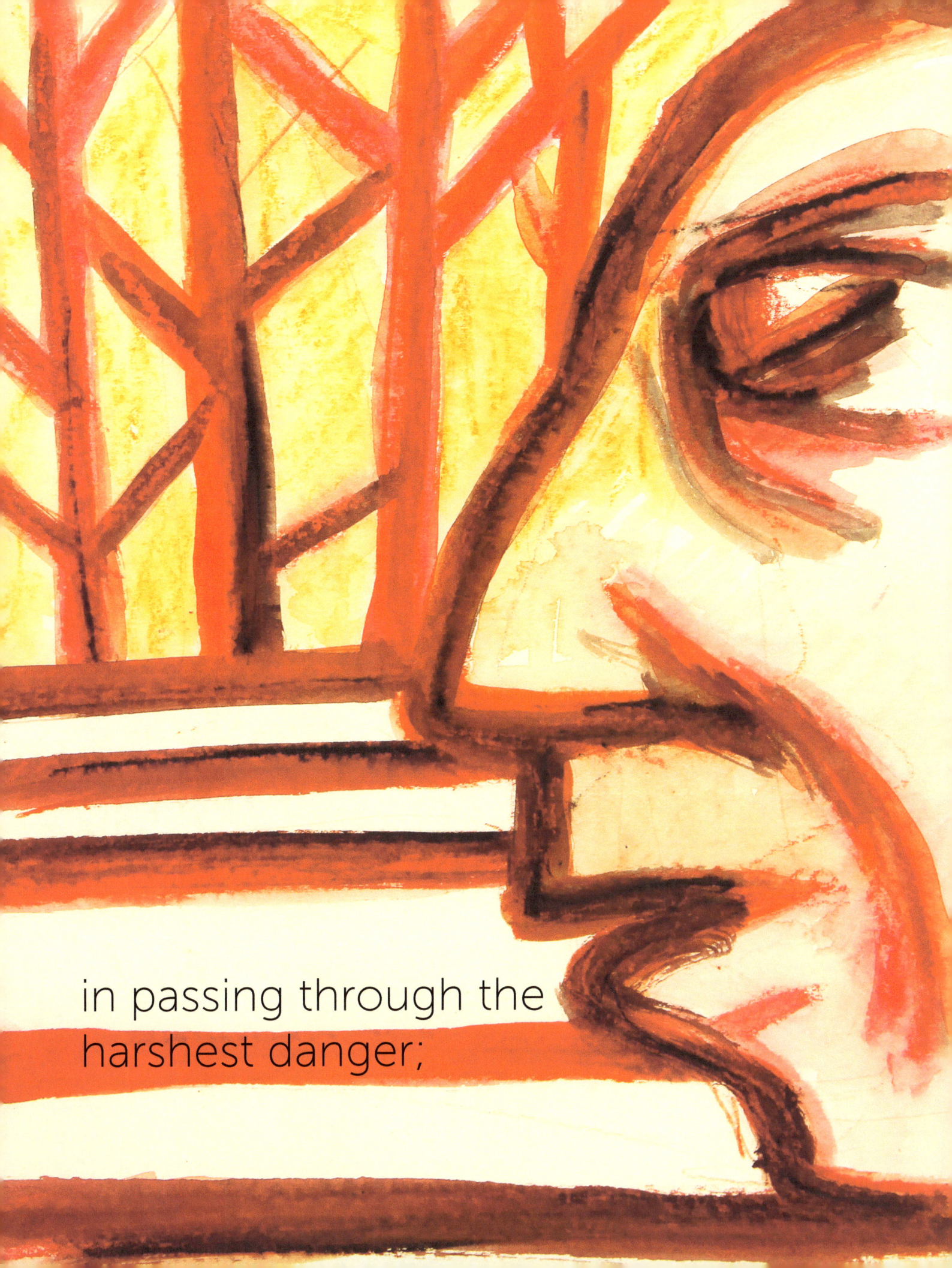

in passing through the
harshest danger;

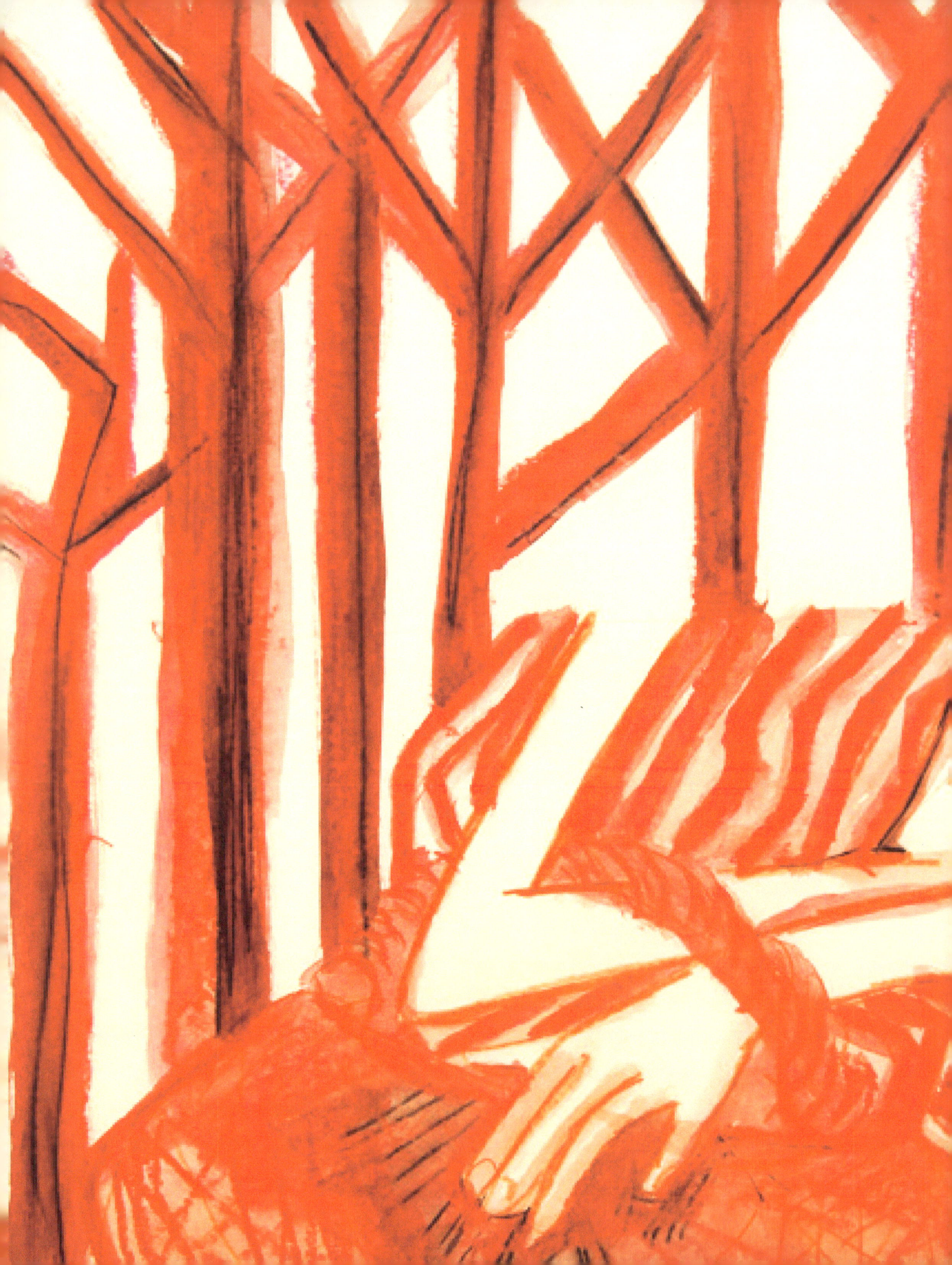

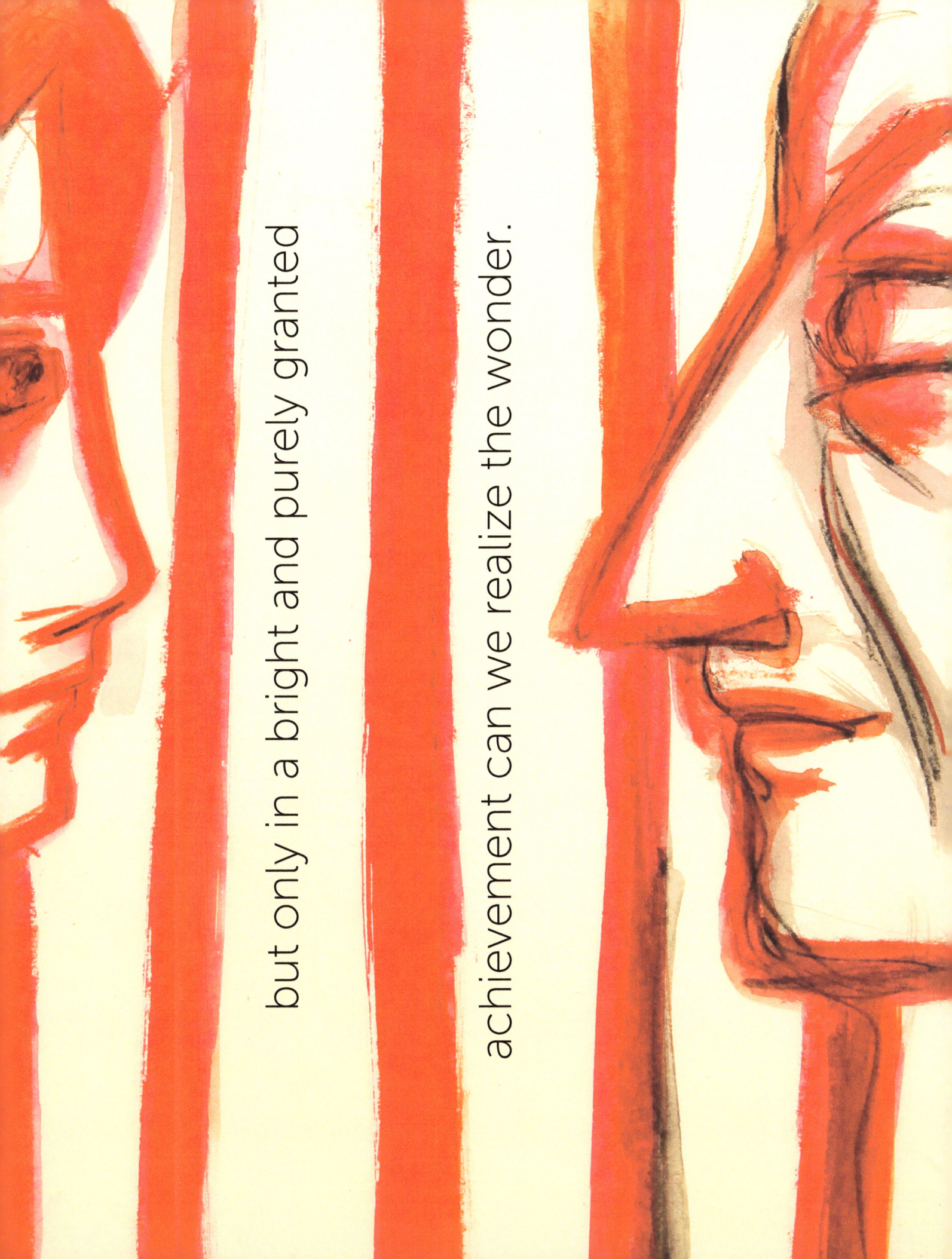

but only in a bright and purely granted

achievement can we realize the wonder.

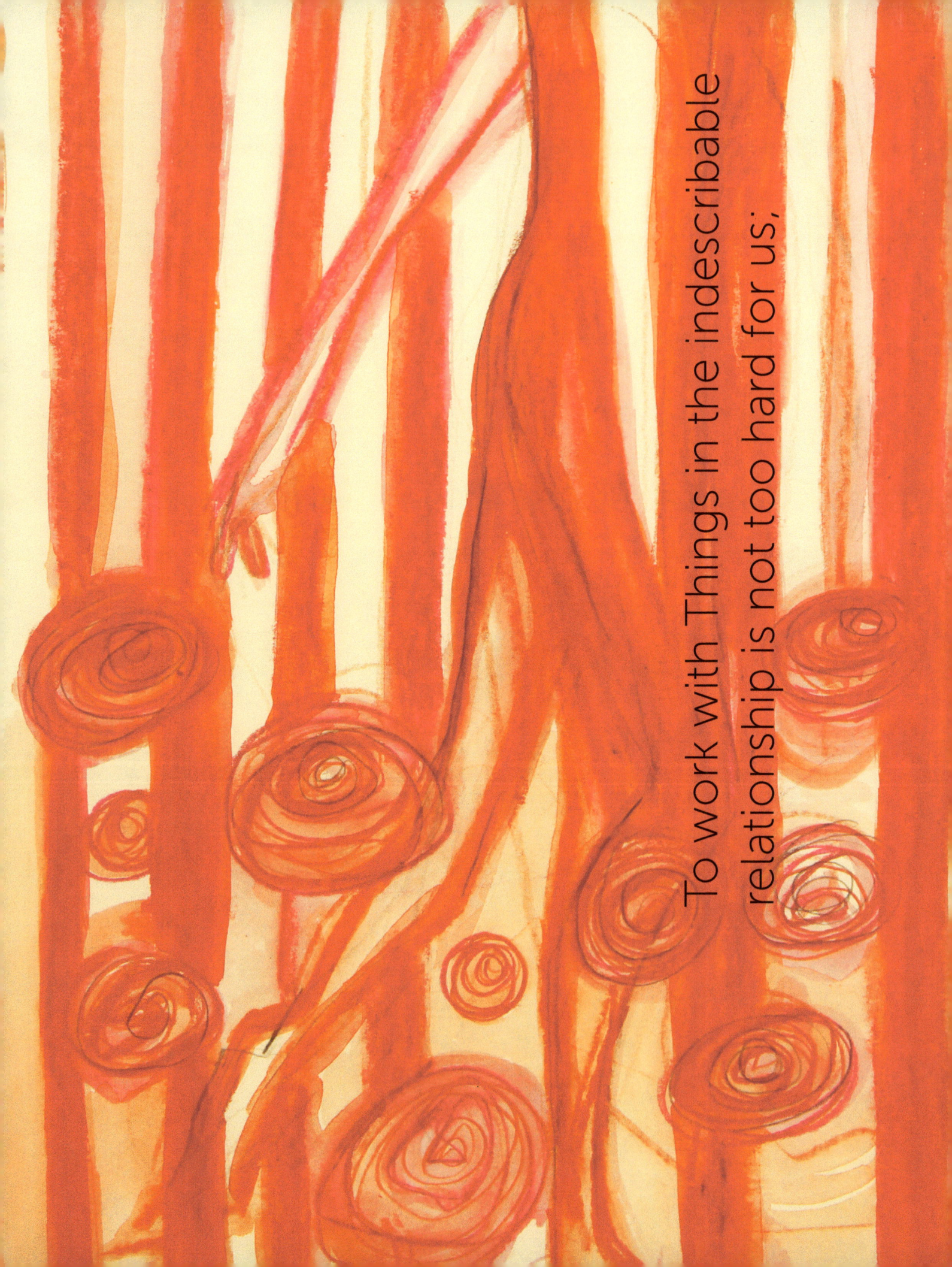

To work with Things in the indescribable relationship is not too hard for us;

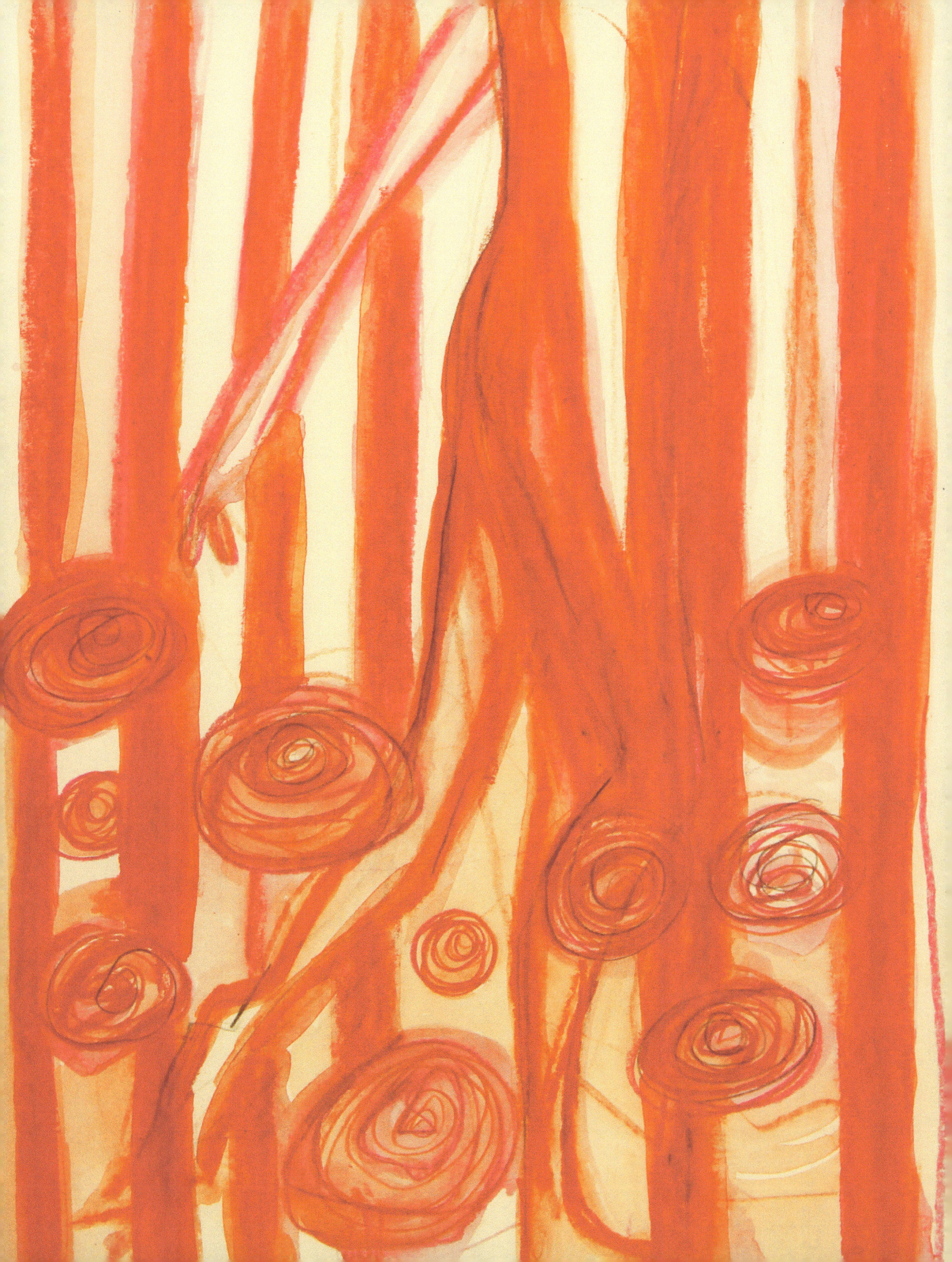

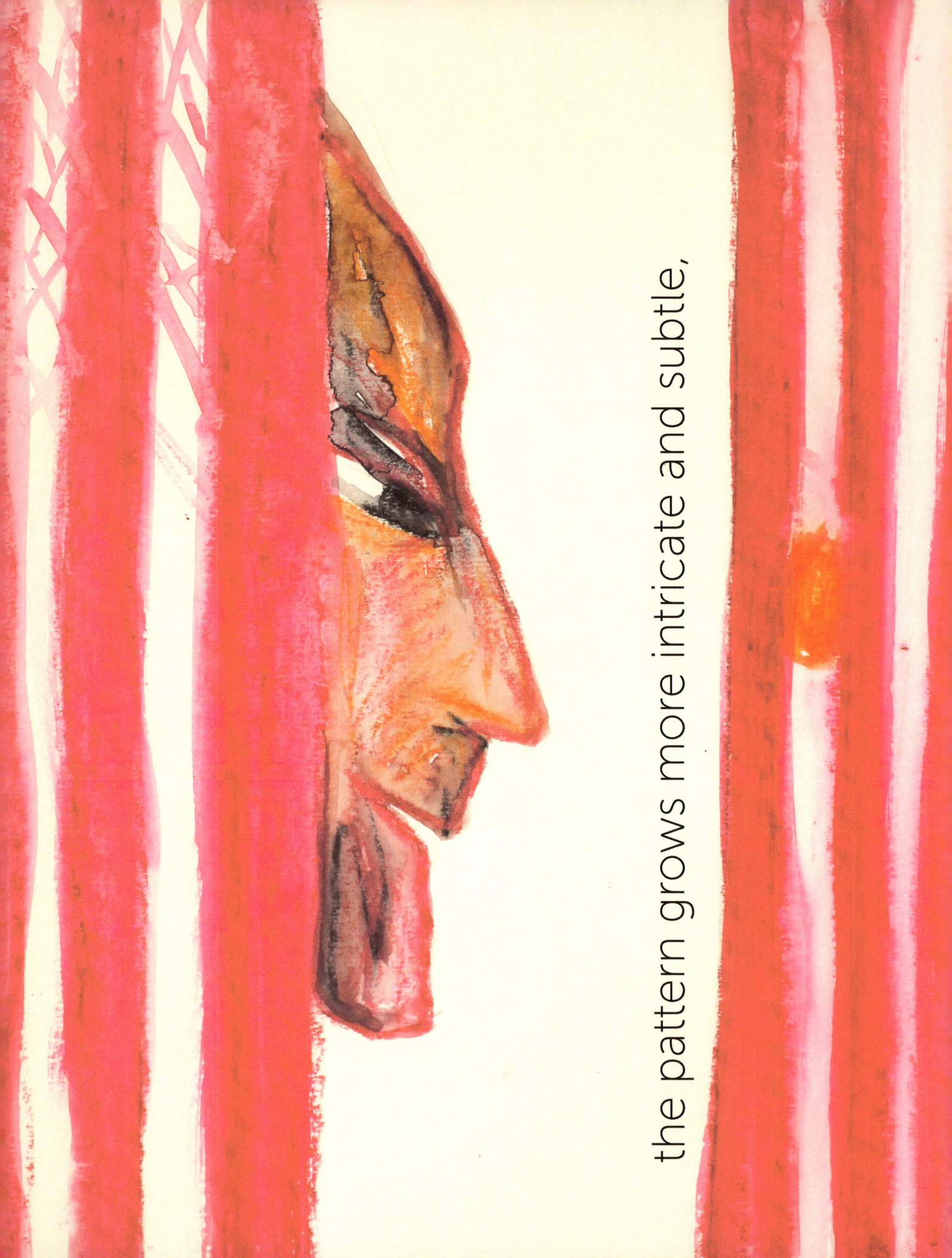

the pattern grows more intricate and subtle,

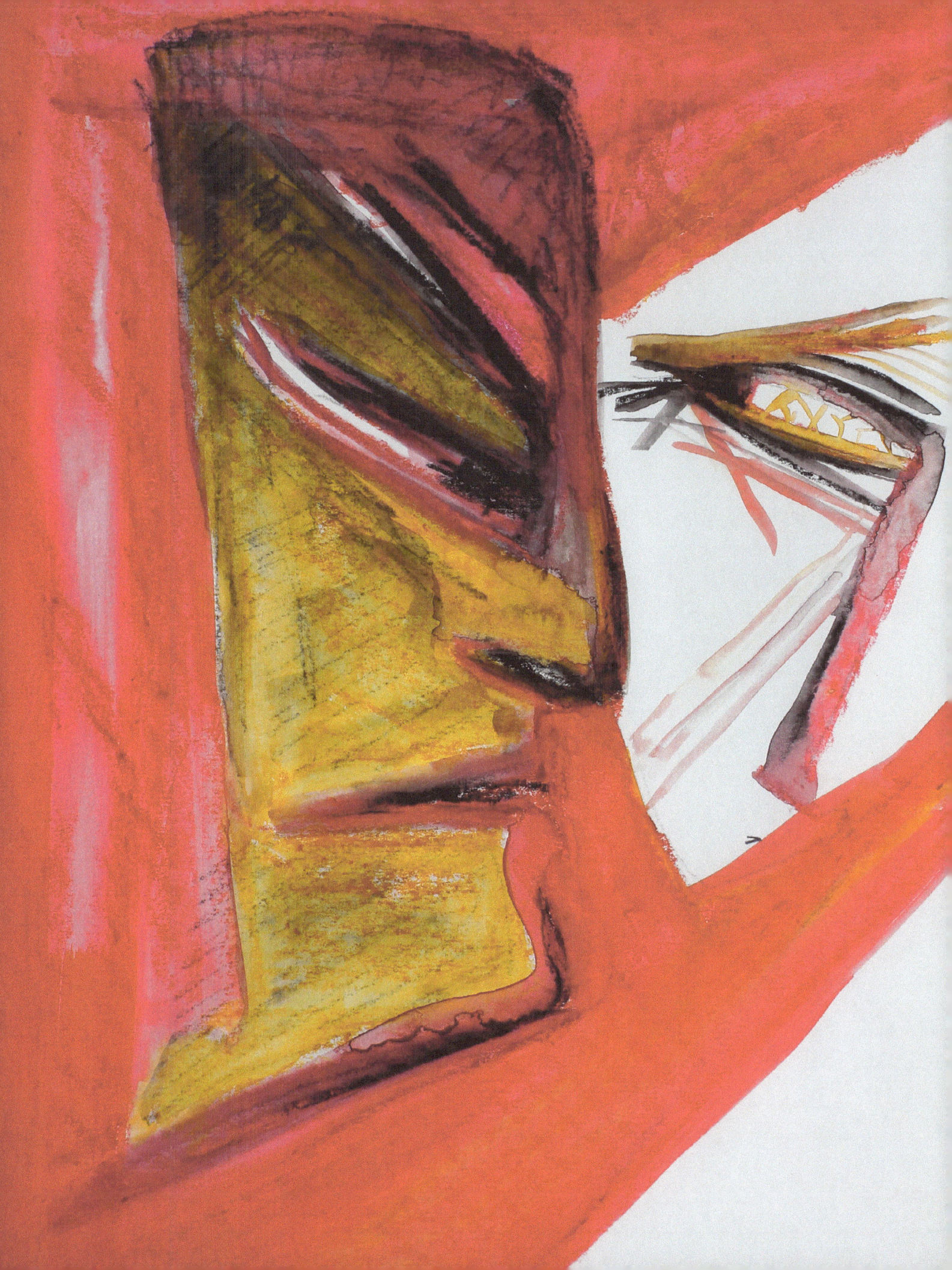

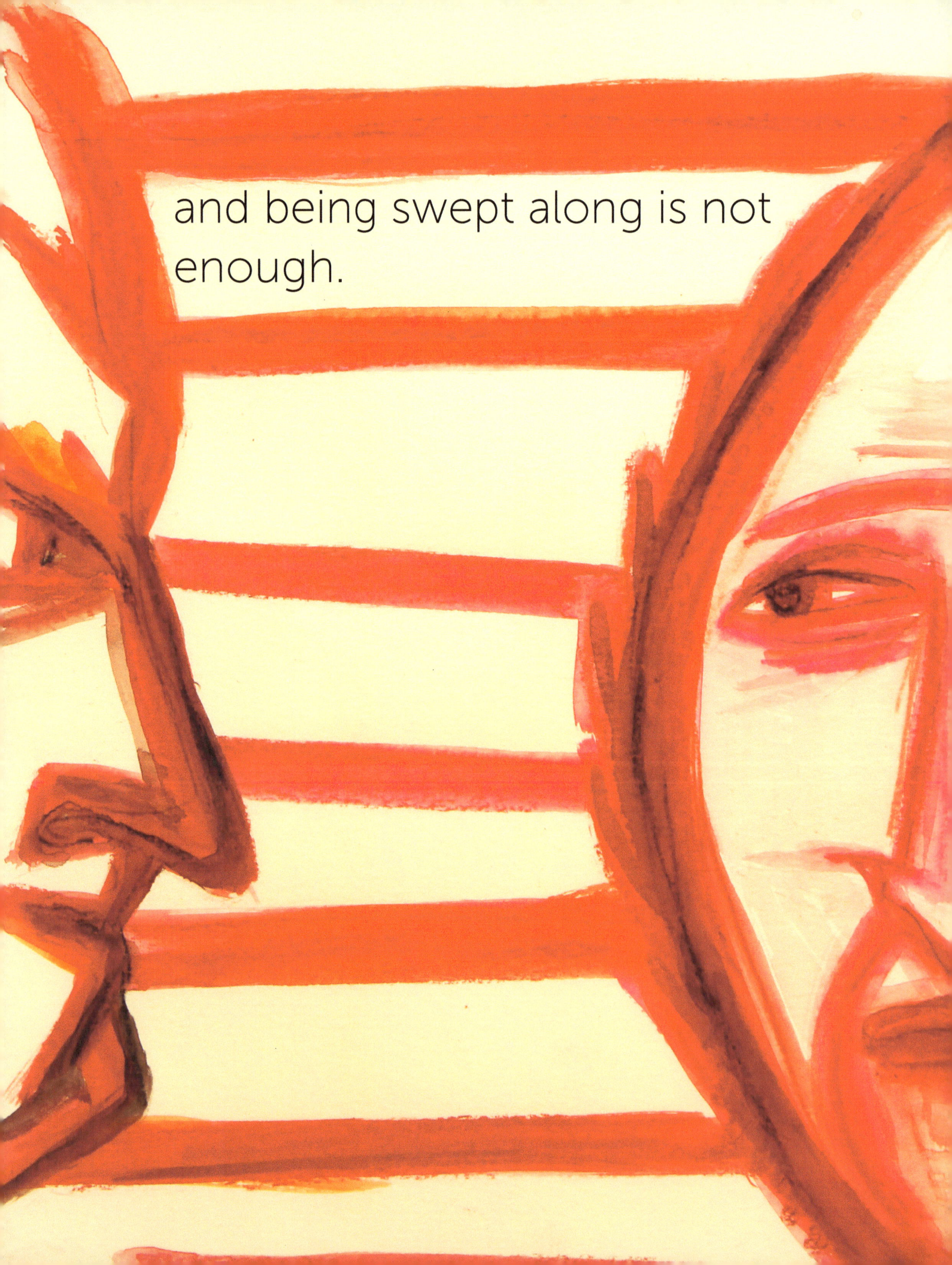

and being swept along is not enough.

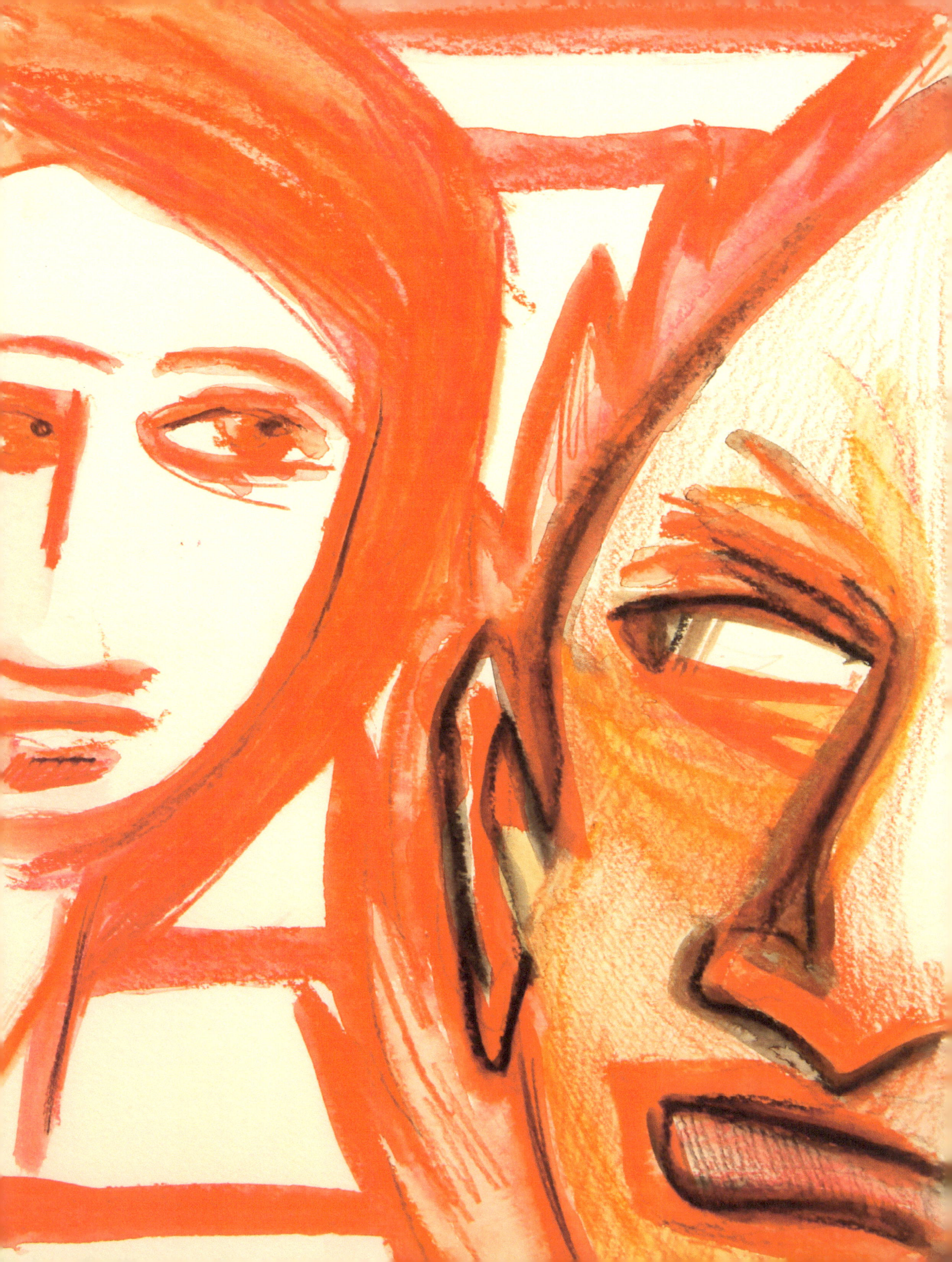

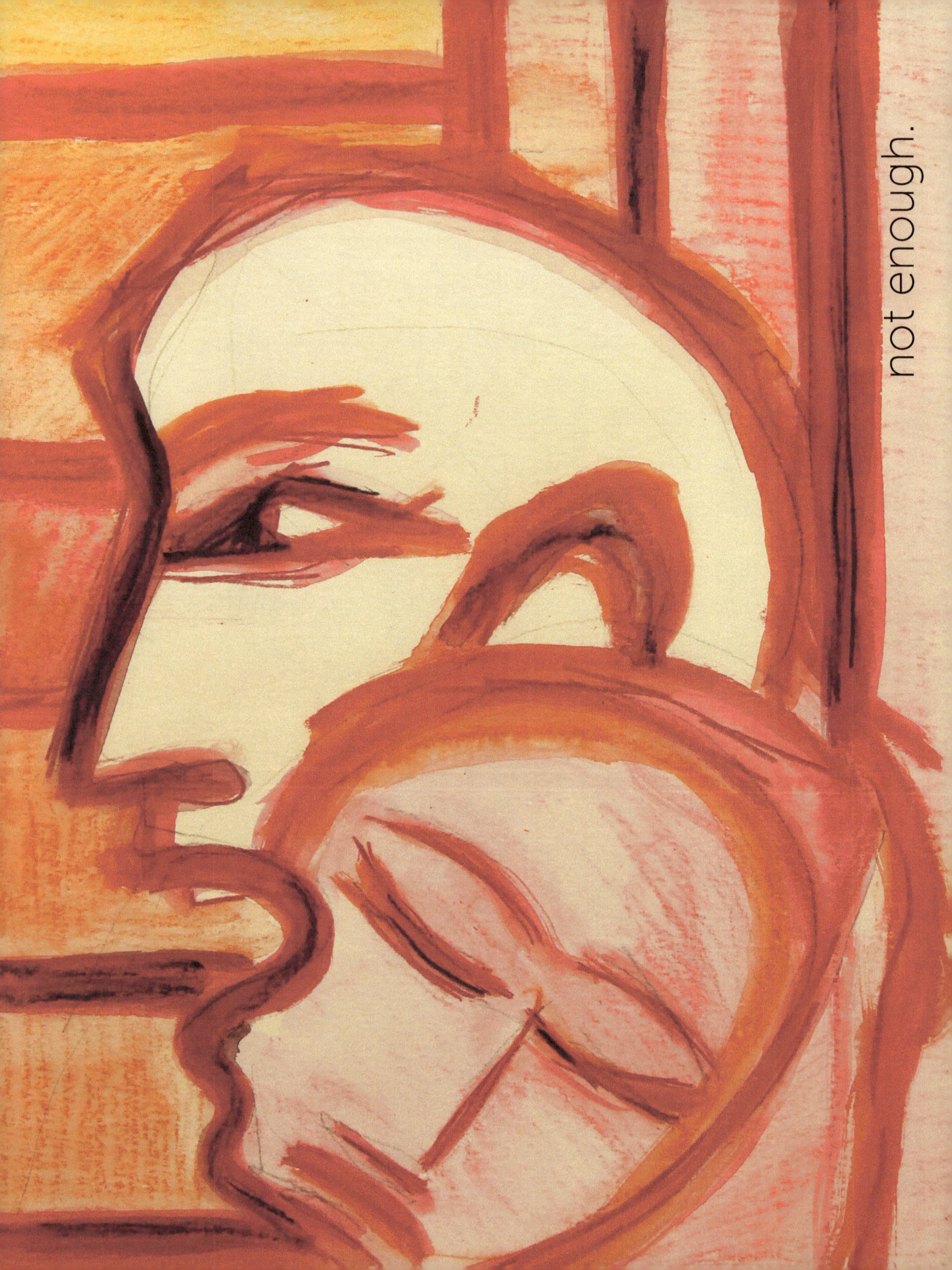

not enough.

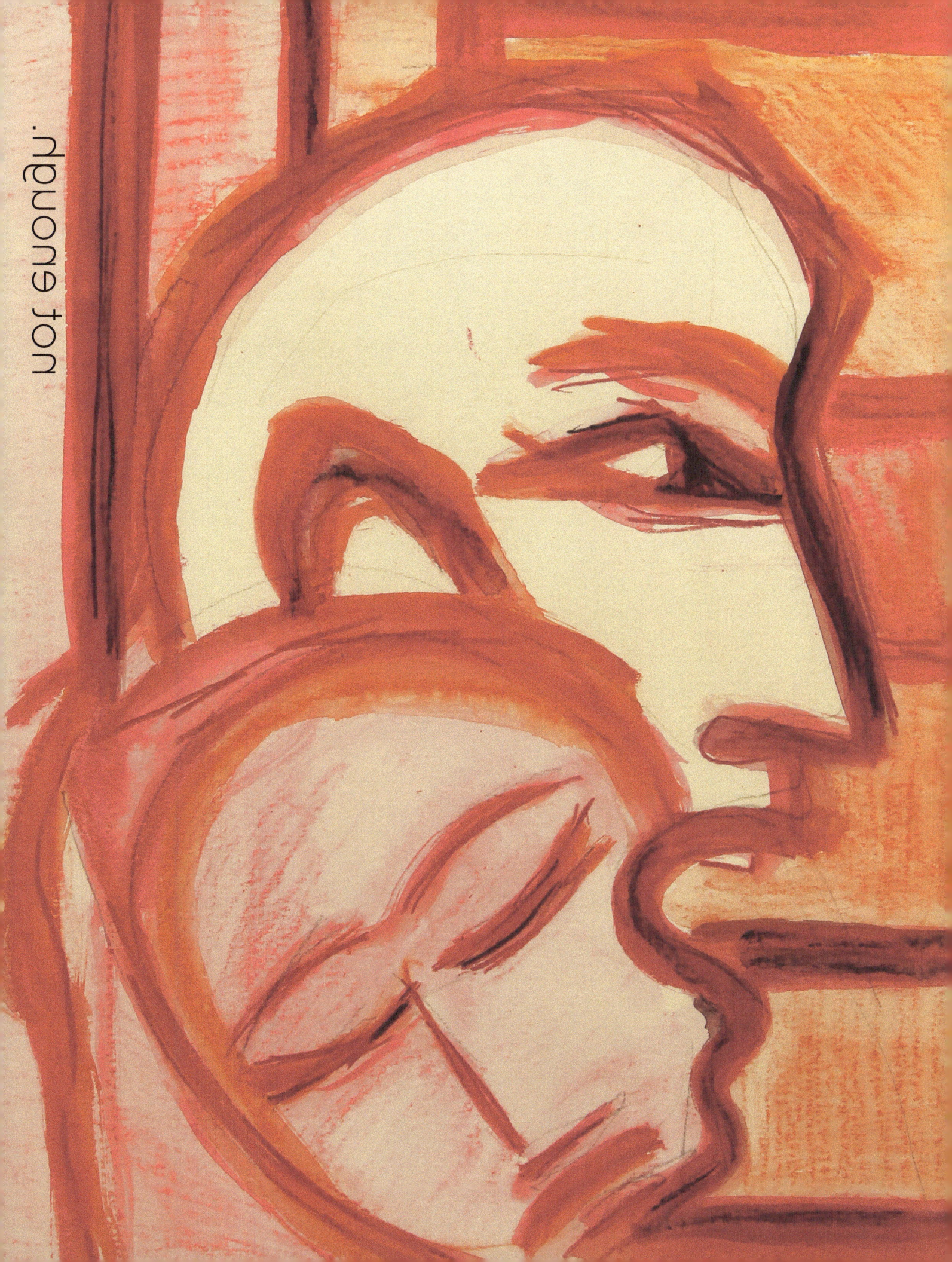

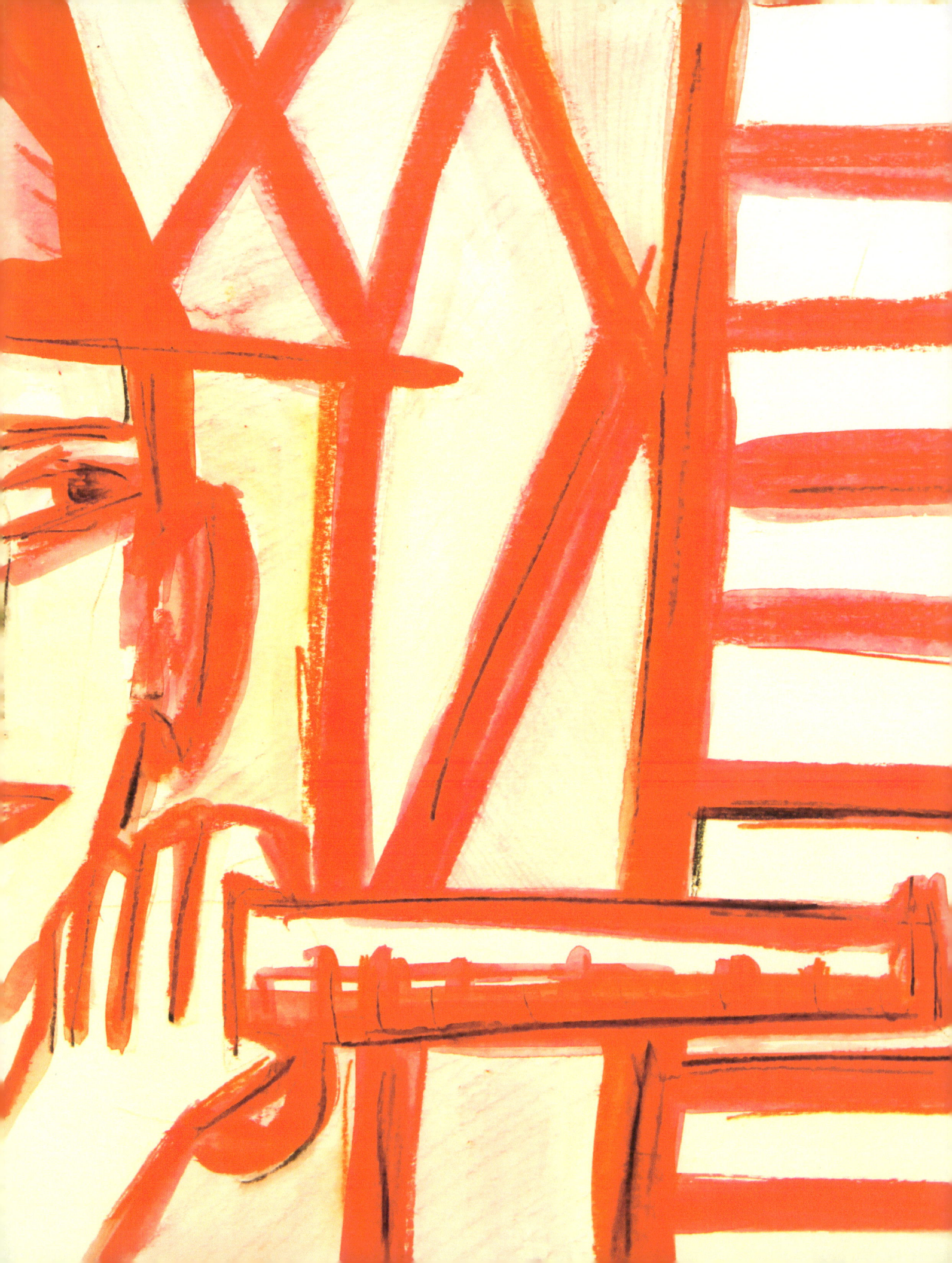

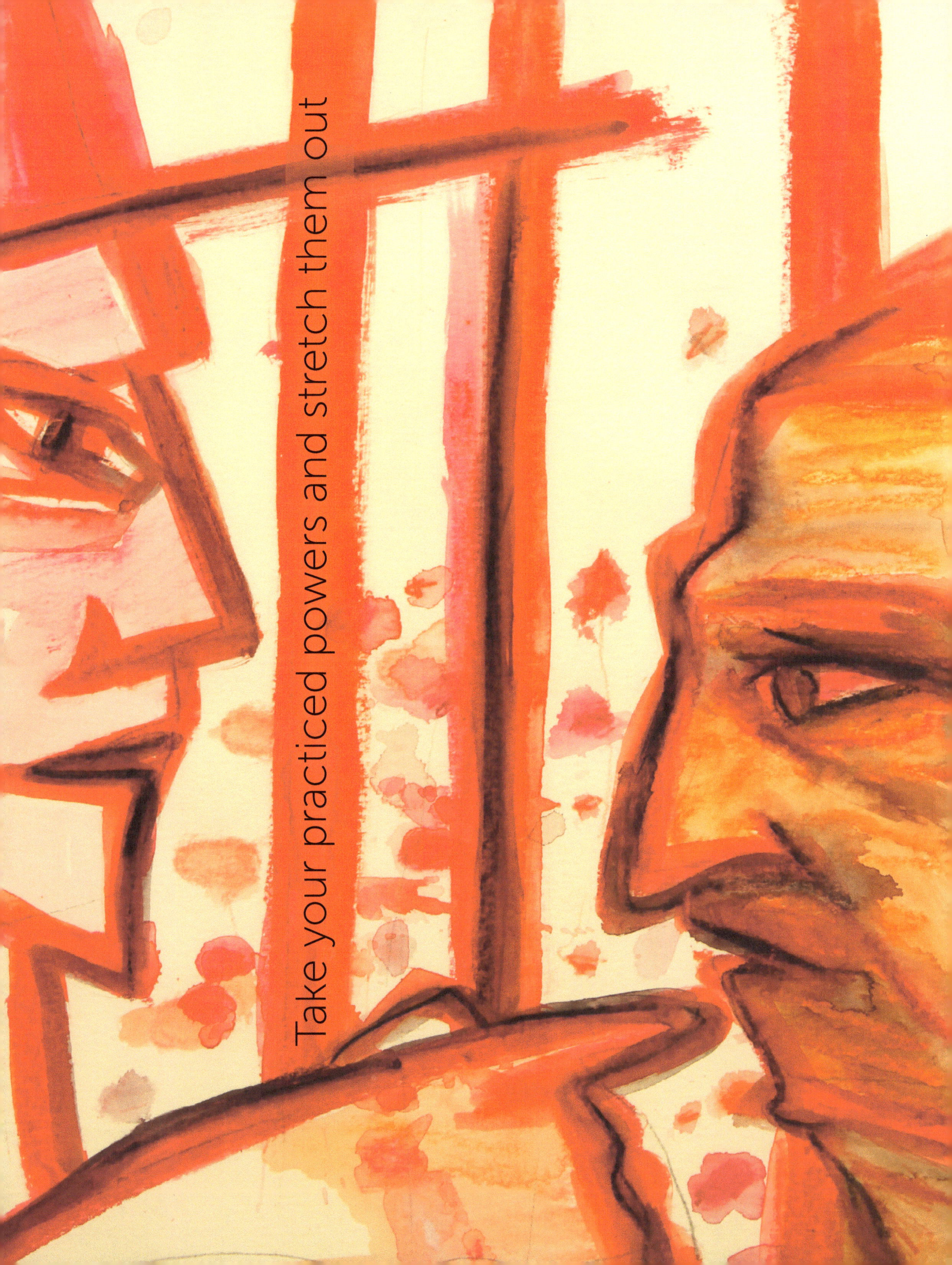

Take your practiced powers and stretch them out

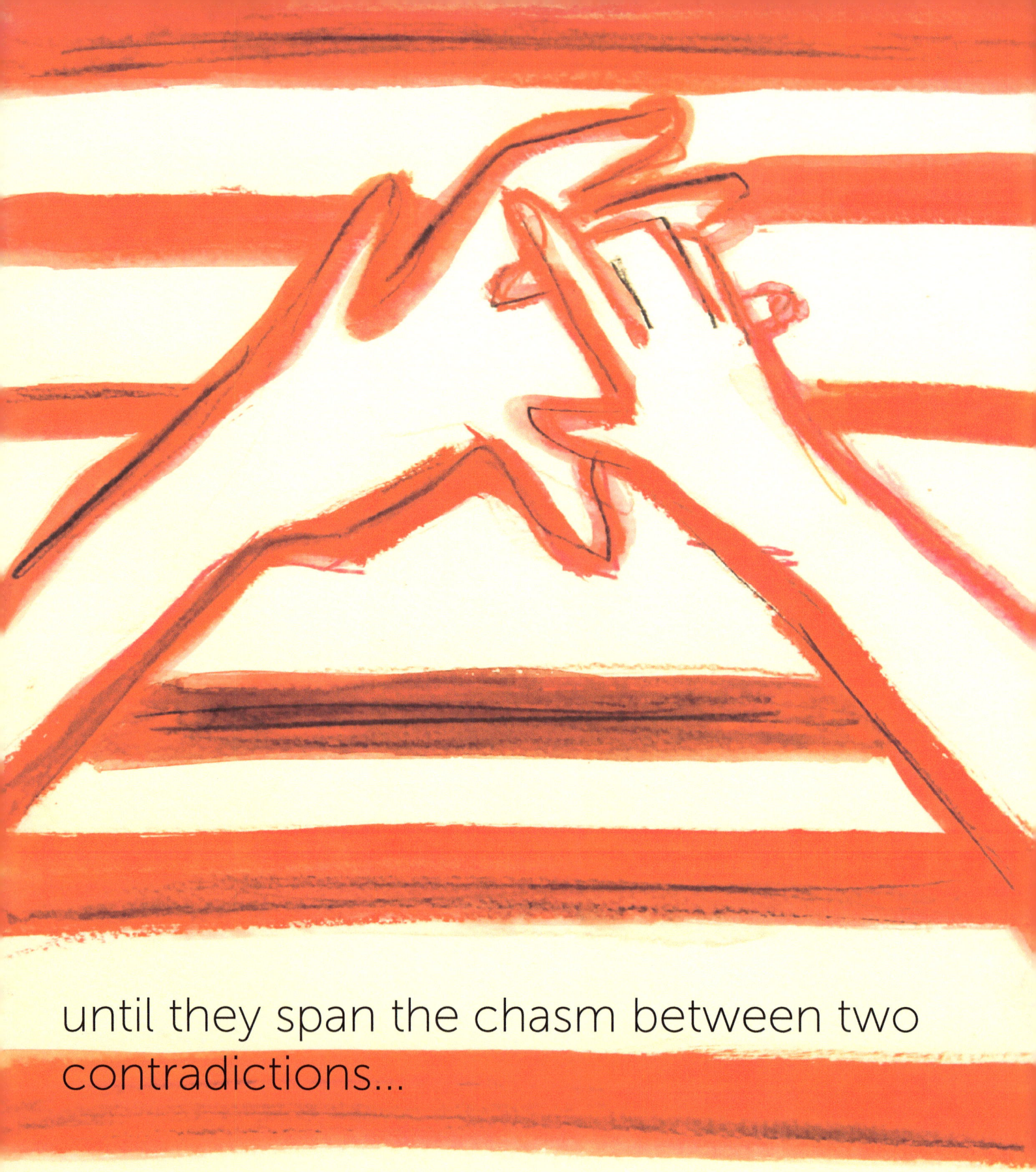

until they span the chasm between two contradictions...

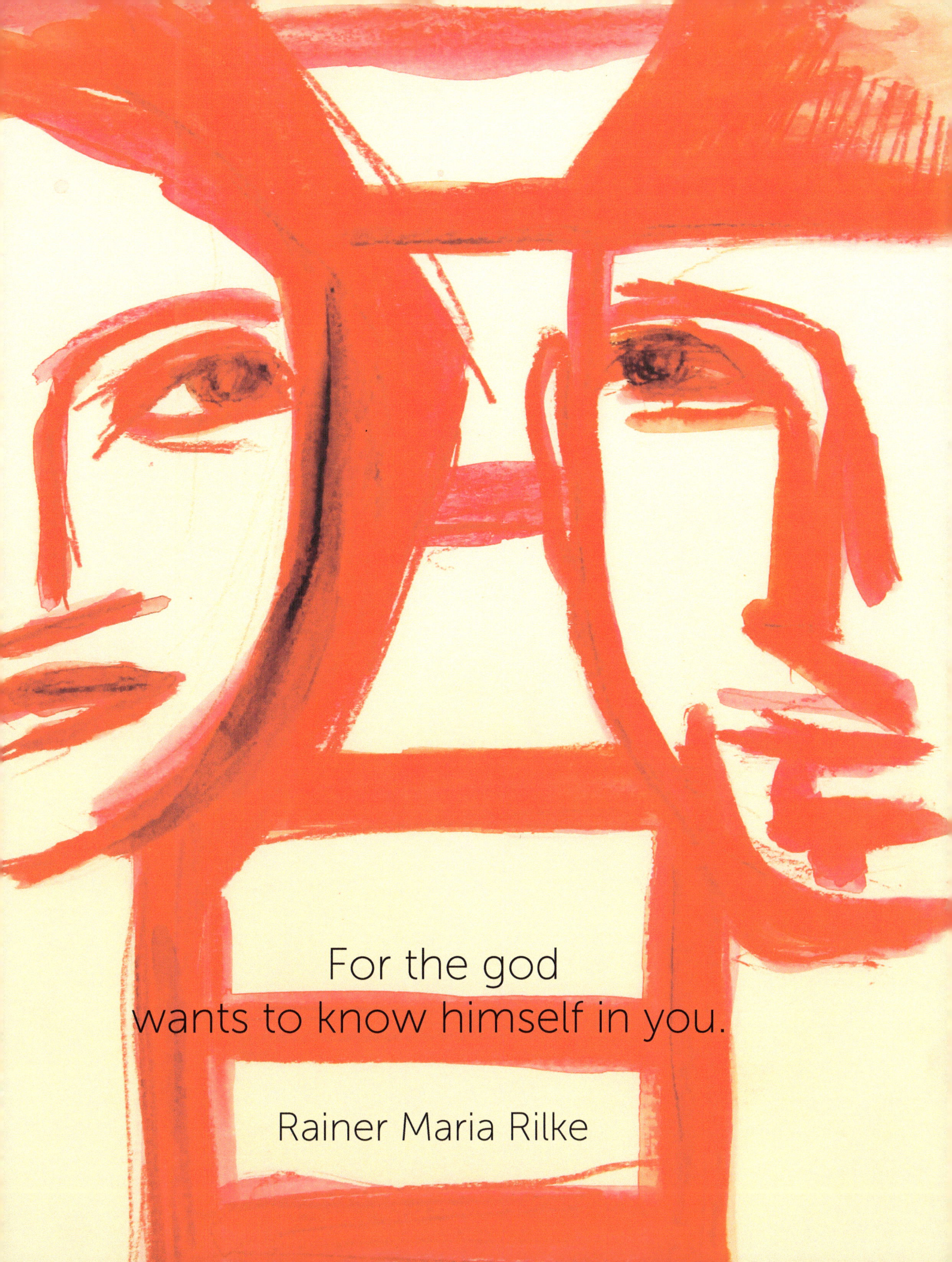

For the god
wants to know himself in you.

Rainer Maria Rilke